Reading is fun!!

Kylar Dietrich

2002

PRESENTED BY

McKamie Jowers

to

Gogi -

thanks for all the shopping

WESTMINSTER SCHOOLS
SMYTHE GAMBRELL LIBRARY

ATLANTA

BY DEBORAH KENT

CHILDREN'S PRESS®
A Division of Grolier Publishing
New York London Hong Kong Sydney
Danbury, Connecticut

CONSULTANTS

Timothy Crimmins
Associate Provost for Academic Programs
Georgia State University, Atlanta

Linda Cornwell
Coordinator of School Quality and Professional Improvement
Indiana State Teachers Association

Project Editor: Downing Publishing Services
Design Director: Karen Kohn & Associates, Ltd.
Photo Researcher: Jan Izzo

Library of Congress Cataloging-in-Publication Data
Kent, Deborah
    Atlanta / by Deborah Kent.
       p. cm. — (Cities of the world)
Includes bibliographical references and index.
Summary: Describes the history, culture, daily life, food, people, sports,
and points of interest in the capital and largest city in the state of Georgia.
    ISBN 0-516-21679-1 (lib. bdg.)   0-516-27282-9(pbk)
    1. Atlanta (Ga.)—Juvenile literature.   [1. Atlanta (Ga.)] I. Title.
II. Series: Cities of the world (New York, N.Y.)
    F294.A84 K46   2000
    975.8'231—dc21
                               00-029450

GROLIER
PUBLISHING

TABLE OF CONTENTS

SOUTH

Summer days can be hot and humid in Atlanta, Georgia. On such days, the Ring Fountain in Centennial Olympic Park is an irresistible lure to young and old. Visitors laugh and shriek as they frolic in the fountain's deliciously cooling spray. Great jets of water shoot as high as 35 feet (10.6 meters) into the air. The fountain's 251 jets are ingeniously arranged to form five interlocking rings, a symbol of the International Olympic Games.

The Ring Fountain and the park in which it stands are a legacy of the Centennial Olympic Games, played in Atlanta in 1996. The Olympics is always a major event, but the 1996 games were a special milestone. The Olympic tradition of the ancient Greeks was revived in 1896, and 1996 was the hundredth anniversary of the Games in modern times. Atlanta had the honor of hosting this Olympic competition.

By some measures, Atlanta was an unusual choice for the Olympic Committee. Never before had the games been played in a city in the southern United States. Never before had they been hosted by a city in which the majority of the population was African American. Atlanta's uniqueness in these areas was not a drawback but an asset. The city is world famous for its role in the movement for black civil rights and nonviolent protest. Furthermore, it is the cultural and economic hub of the southeastern United States. This

Above left: An Olympic pin
Above: Centennial Olympic Park's Ring Fountain at night

A child holding a flag at a Fourth of July parade on Peachtree Street

rapidly developing region is often called the New South.

Atlanta grew at an astonishing rate throughout the twentieth century. That growth took a startling upsurge as the city prepared to receive 8.5 million visitors during the summer of 1996. In the early 1990s, Atlanta launched an all-out construction campaign. The city built new highways, new housing complexes, and a magnificent new stadium. In the years after the Games, these innovations became part of the city itself, and Atlanta continued to grow.

From the beginning, Atlanta has seen itself as a hub of trade. Despite many obstacles, the city has exceeded its early promise. Today, trade flourishes in Atlanta. Its universities, convention centers, and high-tech industries draw people from around the world. As the New South rises, Atlanta lies at its heart.

BEYOND

Anyone who has seen the 1939 movie *Gone with the Wind* will remember Peachtree Street. Peachtree Street was the main thoroughfare in Civil War Atlanta, where much of *Gone with the Wind* takes place. For fans of the movie, the name "Peachtree Street" has a special magic. It carries the flavor of adventure and romance.

Peachtree Street is still one of Atlanta's major avenues. But it bears little resemblance to the street that the film made famous. Today's Peachtree Street passes through the center of a teeming modern city where nearly half a million people live, work, and play. Downtown, the street is lined with forty- and fifty-story skyscrapers instead of white-columned houses.

GETTING TO KNOW ATLANTA

Atlanta has been Georgia's capital since 1868. It lies in the northern part of the state, in the foothills of the Blue Ridge Mountains. The Chattahoochee River forms part of the city's western border. Atlanta expanded rapidly during the twentieth century, engulfing more and more of the land around it. The city proper covers 132 square miles (342 square kilometers), surrounded by an ever-widening sprawl of suburbs.

The section called Downtown Atlanta is at the heart of the metropolis. Here, the gold-domed state capitol stands in contrast to glass-and-steel skyscrapers. Beneath Peachtree Street runs the north-south line of a rapid-rail system with Five Points Station at its hub.

Ducks on the Chattahoochee River

The high-rise towers that loom over Downtown Atlanta extend north along Peachtree Street into the Midtown section. The historic Downtown is experiencing a residential influx, but it is primarily a place devoted to the work of business and government. Most areas of the city, however, are residential. Atlanta is sometimes called the "City of Trees" because many of its neighborhoods have houses with lawns and tree-lined sidewalks.

Above: The Atlanta skyline
Left: The gold-domed state capitol

Some cities are laid out in a careful, gridlike pattern that makes it easy for newcomers to find their way around. Atlanta has no such logical design. Its winding streets, whose names seem to change every two blocks, are a nightmare to out-of-town drivers. Even native Atlantans are often frustrated by the complex layout and the snarls of traffic. Instead of driving, thousands of Atlantans prefer to use the city's network of buses and subways.

Atlantans work in a wide variety of jobs. The majority are employed in service industries—businesses that provide services to groups or individuals. The headquarters of several giant national corporations are located in Atlanta. These companies include United Parcel Service (UPS), Delta Airlines, Holiday Inn, CNN, and Coca-Cola. About half of all Atlantans were born outside the South. Many people move to Atlanta to take jobs with its big corporations.

A view of the Downtown Atlanta skyline and the freeway at dusk

Getting around with MARTA

Atlanta's subway system, known as MARTA (Metropolitan Atlanta Rapid Transit Authority) opened in 1979. By the year 2000, the system had thirty-six stations strung along 30 miles (48 km) of track. Eventually, the system will have 60 miles (97 km) of track and forty-five stations. MARTA also operates bus lines that run throughout the city and into many neighboring suburbs.

"THE CITY TOO BUSY TO HATE"

According to the 1990 census, Atlanta had 394,017 people. The surrounding metropolitan area, however, is far larger, with a population of nearly 3 million. About 40 percent of Georgia's people live in metropolitan Atlanta.

Almost 70 percent of the people who live within the city limits are African Americans. Atlanta has an established black middle class that traces back to the years after the Civil War.

Atlanta University, founded as early as 1867, is the world's largest institution of higher learning for black students. Now called Atlanta University Center, it is a complex of schools including Clark, Spelman, and Morehouse colleges. Atlanta University has

given the city a flourishing community of black professionals.

On the east side of Downtown, the black neighborhood called Sweet Auburn is preserved as a national historic district. Sweet Auburn was the boyhood home of civil-rights leader Dr. Martin Luther King Jr. (1929–1968). The neighborhood has many landmarks of the civil-rights movement.

A former Atlanta mayor, William B. Hartsfield, boasted that the city was "too busy to hate." The phrase became a city slogan. Atlantans are proud of their city's healthy race relations. Public schools and other accommodations integrated peacefully

A young resident of Atlanta

early in the 1960s. However, Atlanta is plagued with the same problems that beset other U.S. cities. Gangs, drugs, and joblessness are rampant in Atlanta's poorest neighborhoods. During the 1980s, Atlanta had the highest per capita murder rate in the nation.

In the 1990s, the city launched a series of crime-prevention programs including anti-drug education and after-school activities for teens. By the end of the decade, the murder rate dropped from 50 to 36 per 100,00 people.

A young Atlanta girl with colorful beads woven into her hair

*These three boys
live in Atlanta's
John Hope Homes.*

LIFE OF THE SPIRIT

On Sunday mornings, Atlanta rings with church bells. The majority of Atlantans are Protestants—Southern Baptists, Methodists, Presbyterians, or other denominations. The city also has many Roman Catholic churches. Some Atlantans worship in Jewish synagogues; others in Islamic mosques.

Churches in Atlanta spearheaded much of the movement for African-American civil rights during the 1950s and 1960s. Black and white ministers rallied their congregations to protest against racial segregation in businesses and schools, on buses and in restaurants. In 1957, Dr. Martin Luther King Jr. founded the Southern Christian Leadership Conference (SCLC). The SCLC brought members of many churches together to work for change. Atlanta has been called the "cradle of the civil-rights movement" because of the work begun by its church leaders.

*A young girl all dressed
up for Sunday school*

THROUGH THEIR GENEROSITY THE DREAM LIVES

DEDICATED TO THE MEMORY OF
DR. MARTIN LUTHER KING, JR.
FOR HIS MORAL COURAGE AND
NOBILITY OF SPIRIT

© MOR

Ebenezer Baptist Church

From 1960 until his death in 1968, Dr. Martin Luther King Jr. was co-pastor of Atlanta's Ebenezer Baptist Church. His father and grandfather before him also were pastors at this church. King's church is now a museum run by the National Park Service. Services are held in the new Ebenezer Baptist Church across the street. Stained-glass windows in the new church depict key moments in the civil-rights struggle.

The phoenix is a bird that appears in the mythology of ancient Greece. Destroyed in a fire, this magical bird springs to life again from its own ashes. In 1888, the city of Atlanta adopted the phoenix as its symbol. Like the phoenix, Atlanta was destroyed by fire and sprang to life once more.

THE TOWN ON THE CHATTAHOOCHEE

When English explorers reached the Chattahoochee River in 1782, they found a thriving village of Cherokee Indians. The explorers wrote that the Cherokee called their village "Standing Peach Tree." However, historians point out that peach trees were not native to northern Georgia. They suggest that the name may have been a misspelling of "Standing Pitch Tree," a reference to the pitch pines that are common in the region. Whatever the case, the peach tree has had a close connection with Atlanta since the city's beginnings.

During the War of 1812, when the United States fought Great Britain, the Americans built Fort Peach Tree on the site of the old Cherokee village. After the war, the fort became the center of a growing white settlement. Though Fort Peach Tree was only a remote frontier outpost, some village leaders felt it had great possibilities. Perhaps it could become a hub of trade, with puffing locomotives carrying goods in and out along shining tracks. The Georgia legislature established the Western & Atlantic Railroad in 1837, proposing Fort Peach Tree as its southernmost terminal. The name of the town was changed from Fort Peach Tree to Terminus. The name changed again in 1843, to Marthasville, in honor of the daughter of former Georgia governor Wilson Lumpkin.

Slave quarters on an Atlanta plantation

An Atlanta woman at the market is accompanied by a house slave.

The Peach Tree Mystique

Peachtree Street, Peachtree Court, Peachtree Plaza, Peachtree Center. "Peachtree" appears in the names of thirty-two Atlanta streets and landmarks. Peaches were a major crop in the Atlanta region until the 1920s. Today, the peanut is far more important to the area's economy. But no one is eager to update Atlanta place names. How would it sound to say Peanut Street, Peanut Court, and Peanut Center? Somehow it just wouldn't be the same!

The first Western & Atlantic locomotive, the Kentucky, steamed into Marthasville in 1845. The town was definitely on the rise. Once again, leaders felt that a change of name was in order. J. Edgar Thomson, the railroad's chief engineer, suggested the name Atlanta. No one knows for sure where the name came from, but it may have derived from "Atlantic" in the name Western & Atlantic. No matter where it came from, Atlanta proved to be a name that would last.

Atlanta depended on slaves
to work in the fields and pick
the cotton crop.

A cotton ball

Slaves picking cotton

During the Civil War, Atlanta women volunteered as nurses.

"WAR IS HELL"

From the town's earliest days, slavery was part of life in Atlanta. Slavery was embedded in the economy of Georgia, as it was throughout the southern states. Conflict over slavery divided the northern and southern states during the 1850s, and finally led to civil war. In 1861, Georgia seceded from the United States and became part of a new nation, the Confederate States of America. Atlanta made a bid to become the Confederate capital but was passed over in favor of Richmond, Virginia.

During the Civil War (1861–1865), Atlanta contributed iron and cloth to the Confederacy. As the war pressed close to home, trainloads of sick and wounded soldiers poured into the city every day. Hundreds of Atlanta women volunteered as nurses, though sometimes they could do little more than speak words of comfort and hold the hand of a dying man.

The Battle of Atlanta began in 1864 when Union general William Tecumseh Sherman received orders to penetrate the interior of Georgia and South Carolina. Commanding General Ulysses S. Grant ordered Sherman to "inflict as much damage as you can against their resources." Sherman had as his target the railroad connections of the lower South. At their center stood Atlanta. Because his military objectives included capturing centers of civilian population, Sherman is said to have coined the phrase, "War is hell."

As a young U.S. Army lieutenant in 1844, Sherman was stationed in Marthasville for two months.

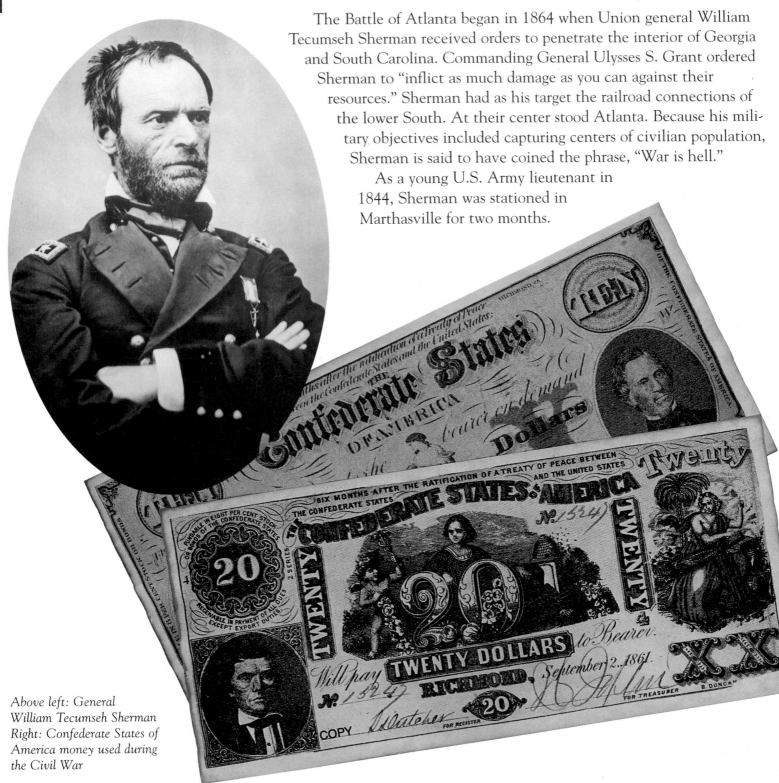

Above left: General William Tecumseh Sherman Right: Confederate States of America money used during the Civil War

Twenty years later, Sherman vividly remembered the city's layout. His knowledge of Atlanta's streets, bridges, and railroad tracks was invaluable as he planned his campaign against the city. The assault began in July with the Battle of Peachtree Creek and continued throughout the summer. In one clash after another, Atlanta's defenders under General John Bell Hood suffered terrible losses. Yet they refused to accept defeat.

Confederate soldiers on guard at the edge of Atlanta in 1864

The World's Biggest Painting

During the 1890s, eleven artists created an extraordinary painting called *The Battle of Atlanta*. Commonly known as the *Cyclorama*, the painting is a giant cylinder 42 feet (13 m) high and 358 feet (109 m) around. As the cylinder revolves, viewers see the story of the battle unfold scene by scene. Located inside this building in Grant Park, the *Cyclorama* is one of Atlanta's most popular attractions.

One of the bloodiest battles for Atlanta occurred on August 9. An eyewitness described it as "that red day when all the fires of hell and all the thunders of the universe seemed to be blazing and roaring over Atlanta." By then, food supplies were running low, and Atlantans were growing desperate. Some abandoned their homes and retreated to the countryside to escape the shelling and the constant fear.

After Sherman's troops cut the last railroad link to the outside, the Confederate forces abandoned the city. On September 2, 1864, civilians fled as Union soldiers poured through the streets.

In wagons or on foot, families escaped with whatever they could carry. Loaded with clothing, pots and pans, family portraits, and even live chickens, they clogged the streets in their frantic haste.

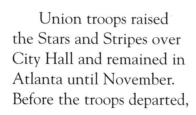

CSA (Confederate States of America) pin and buttons

Union troops raised the Stars and Stripes over City Hall and remained in Atlanta until November. Before the troops departed,

they set fire to the railroad and commercial buildings at the heart of the city. Towers of flame engulfed street after street. When the Union soldiers marched out of the city, only one in ten of Atlanta's houses and other buildings were left standing.

Union general William Tecumseh Sherman watching troop movements through a pair of binoculars

General Sherman and his Union troops destroyed Atlanta.

*Atlanta citizens fleeing ahead of
General Sherman's relentless march*

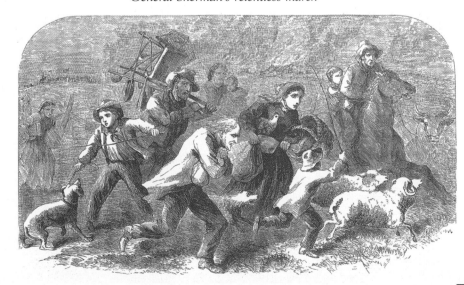

BUILDING A FUTURE

When the Civil War was over, Atlantans set to work rebuilding their ruined city. Once again, trains chugged through the city and rumbling wagons clogged the streets. This time, the wagons were loaded with lumber and bricks. Work crews labored feverishly to construct new houses, churches, and other buildings. Like the mythical phoenix, Atlanta sprang up from its ashes, stronger than ever before.

In 1868, Atlanta became the capital of Georgia. With its train lines and its rising businesses, Atlanta had many advantages over the previous capital, Milledgeville. Atlanta's domed state capitol, completed in 1889, had the classical details of the U.S. Capitol. It symbolized the return of the state to the Union.

Bustling Atlanta as it looked in 1887

Atlanta was growing rapidly, and in 1880 it had 37,000 people. Henry Grady, an Atlanta newspaper editor, wrote in 1886 that the southern states were setting aside the past and striding toward the twentieth century. This was the "New South," Grady proclaimed, and Atlanta lay at its heart.

As Atlanta grew, black people and white people took pride in their city. People of both races felt hopeful about the future.

W. E. B. Du Bois, a professor at Atlanta University, helped to found the National Association for the Advancement of Colored People (NAACP). For decades, the NAACP worked to widen opportunities for African Americans throughout the United States. Atlanta remained an important regional center for this organization.

Civic leaders gave Atlantans a lasting gift in 1904 by creating Piedmont Park just north of Downtown. But Atlanta suffered a stunning blow in 1917 when fire ravaged 73 square blocks of the city.

In 1917, a devastating fire destroyed 73 square blocks of Atlanta.

W. E. B. Du Bois

Once again, Atlantans hurled themselves into the enormous task of rebuilding. Like the phoenix, Atlanta rose from its ashes for a second time.

During World War II, factories in Atlanta made parts for weapons, ships, and aircraft. A naval air station opened in the nearby town of Chamblee in 1943.

Atlanta's growth took a giant leap in 1952, as the city annexed 81 square miles (210 sq km) of its surrounding suburbs. Overnight, the population zoomed with an additional 100,000 people. To ease the flow of traffic, Atlanta built a network of expressways across the sprawling city. As Atlanta spread outward, business and civic leaders sought to revitalize the downtown area. Peachtree Plaza, an immense complex of shops, restaurants, hotels, office towers, and convention space, opened in the 1960s.

Atlanta was a strictly segregated city until the 1960s, when the public schools and other facilities were peacefully integrated.

Maynard Jackson and his wife, Bunie, celebrat[e] Jackson's election as mayor of Atlanta.

The Civil War put an end to slavery, but it did not bring true freedom to Atlanta's African Americans. Black people still endured the crushing effects of racial discrimination. In the first half of the twentieth century, black people and white people attended separate schools, sat in separate rows on buses, drank from separate public fountains, and dined in separate restaurants. In the 1950s and 1960s, pioneering civil-rights leaders pushed for racial equality. With relatively little turmoil, Atlanta became a fully integrated city. It set an example for other cities around the country. Despite Atlanta's reputation for racial harmony, however, black people still had little voice in city government. Atlanta finally elected its first African-American mayor, Maynard Jackson, in 1974.

When Atlanta was selected to host the Centennial Olympic Games in 1996, some citizens worried about the crowding, the commercialism, and the strain on city services. But excitement mounted as the city's preparations got underway. Atlantans tried to present the world with a strong, positive image of their city.

The Centennial Olympics proved to be a gala celebration of athletic skill and international cooperation. Tragedy struck during the contests. A terrorist's bomb exploded in Centennial Olympic Park, killing two people and injuring dozens of others. Atlantans and their guests refused to give in to terror tactics. The day after the blast, the Games resumed according to plan. In the spirit of the phoenix, Atlanta rose again, undefeated, determined to move on.

Things Go Better with Coke

In 1886, an Atlanta druggist named John S. Pemberton began selling a sweet, fizzy drink as a remedy for headaches. The concoction tasted so good that customers asked for it even when they felt well. Pemberton called his creation Coca-Cola. After a few years, he sold his business, which went on to dazzling national and later international success. Today, Atlanta's Coca-Cola Museum includes a replica of Jacobs' Pharmacy, where the first Coke was served.

Study and work are a way of life in Atlanta. Emory University, Atlanta University, Georgia Institute of Technology (Georgia Tech), Georgia State University, and other schools of higher learning play a key role in the life of the city. Atlantans work at a wide variety of jobs—in high-tech industries, manufacturing, and sales, and for state and federal agencies.

When they are not at work or at school, Atlantans are always busy. They enjoy music, the arts, sports, and the outdoors. Atlanta provides abundant opportunities for its people to play when work and study are done.

LISTENING IN

On summer days, Piedmont Park is alive with joggers, cyclists, romping children, and barking dogs. On concert evenings, the atmosphere is transformed. Thousands of people sit quietly on folding chairs or sprawl on blankets on the grass. Everyone grows still to hear the strains of the music. Whether the concert is a gospel choir or a jazz quintet, a rock band or a symphony orchestra, it finds a devoted audience in Atlanta.

Atlanta's nightclubs offer an array of musical options from country to jazz to rock. Many of these clubs are located in the Downtown complex known as Underground Atlanta. While many gospel choirs sing profes- sionally, some of the best gospel music can be heard during Sunday church services.

Lovers of classical music can attend concerts by the Atlanta Symphony Orchestra. The orchestra plays in the 1,700-seat

Atlantans enjoying Piedmont Park

Symphony Hall in Woodruff Arts Center located on Peachtree Street, 3 miles (4.8 km) north of Downtown. The Atlanta Symphony performed for the first time in 1944.

Also immensely popular with classical music buffs is the Atlanta Opera. The Atlanta Opera Company gives four productions a year at Fox Theater. Other musical events in the city include performances by the Atlanta Chamber Players and the Atlanta Ballet.

One of the entrances to Underground Atlanta

Dancing on Strings

In 1978, an unusual host inaugurated one of the most unique museums in Atlanta. The museum was the Center for Puppetry, and the host at the gala ceremony was none other than Kermit the Frog. Galleries at the museum display hand puppets and marionettes from around the world. Visitors can even try working the strings themselves and making some of these intricate figures leap and dance. Puppet shows are staged regularly in the center's 300-seat theater.

LOOKING AT PICTURES

Atlanta's High Museum of Art is a study in white. On the outside, the building is sheathed in sparkling white ceramic tiles. The building is white on the inside as well, giving it a sense of airiness and space. With a collection of some 10,000 works, the High is the finest art museum in Atlanta. Its four floors of galleries include photographs, American paintings, decorative arts, and sculpture from sub-Saharan Africa. Swinging above the museum's front lawn is a spectacular giant mobile by sculptor Alexander Calder.

Art objects from around the world are on display at the Michael C. Carlos Museum of Emory University. The museum's core collection is a group of paintings and sculptures gathered by Emory professors of the nineteenth century on their travels to Africa, the Near East, and the South Seas. The Callanwold Fine Arts Center is housed in the 1920 mansion of Coca-Cola heir Charles Howard Candler. As a legacy to Atlanta, Candler left his home to be used as an art school where adults and children can take classes.

A dazzling collection of pieces by African Americans is on exhibit at Hammond's House Galleries and Resource Center. The center occupies the 1867 home of Otis T. Hammond, a black doctor who had a deep love of the arts. In addition to work by African Americans, Hammond's House displays art from Africa and the Caribbean. The center's research library is a treasure-house for anyone interested in the contributions of African-American artists.

The High Museum of Art

General Robert E. Lee (right) is one of the leaders of the Confederacy depicted on the enormous Stone Mountain sculpture (above).

ROBERT E. LEE

Stone Mountain Park lies a few miles from Atlanta. There, the great outdoors serves as a gallery for the biggest bas-relief sculpture on earth. Carved from a massive granite outcropping, the sculpture portrays three leaders of the Confederacy: President Jefferson Davis and Generals Stonewall Jackson and Robert E. Lee, each mounted on horseback. Gutzon Borglum, best known for his carvings of U.S. presidents at Mount Rushmore, South Dakota, began the Stone Mountain project in 1923. After ten painstaking years with pick and chisel, Borglum left the work unfinished. The figures were finally completed in 1970 by sculptors Walter Kirtland Hancock and Roy Faulkner.

Home of the Braves

Turner Field (right), where the Braves play their home games, was originally designed for the Centennial Olympics of 1996. It is not merely a stadium, but a celebration of the Braves and their history. At the Braves Museum and Hall of Fame, visitors marvel at the bats, mitts, and uniforms of their favorite players, or watch videos of classic games. Drop in at the East Pavilion to get a personalized baseball card, featuring your own photo.

ATLANTA SCORES!

Professional sports is a true passion in Atlanta. The Atlanta area is represented by the Atlanta Hawks (pro basketball), the Atlanta Falcons (pro football), and the Atlanta Braves (National League baseball). The Braves moved to Atlanta from Milwaukee in 1966. With them came Henry (Hank) Aaron, their remarkable star outfielder. In 1974, Aaron broke a record many baseball fans thought would never be eclipsed. He smashed the 715th home run of his career, topping the mark set years earlier by baseball legend Babe Ruth. When Aaron finally retired, he had hit 755 regular season homers, earning him a place in baseball's Hall of Fame.

In many respects, the Atlanta Braves were the most successful baseball team of the 1990s. During that decade, they won more games and scored more runs than any other team. Pitching was the key to their success. Crafty hurlers such as Greg Maddux and John Smoltz led the Braves to victory after victory. However, the team's success was marred by disappointments in World Series contests. During the 1990s, the Braves went to the coveted World Series five times but emerged as champions only once, in 1995.

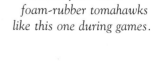

Braves fans wave foam-rubber tomahawks like this one during games.

Hall of Fame Atlanta Braves outfielder Henry Aaron

The Georgia Dome, which seats 71,500 spectators, is home to the Atlanta Falcons, the city's National Football League (NFL) team. The 1998–99 Atlanta Falcons advanced to the Super Bowl, only to lose to the Denver Broncos. The Georgia Dome was the scene of the Super Bowl contests in 1994 and 2000.

Atlantans are dedicated fans of all their professional teams. They are also loyal to their leading college team, the Yellowjackets from the Georgia Institute of Technology. Formerly known as the Ramblin' Wrecks, they play at Dodd-Grant Field in Atlanta's Grant Park. Old-time fans love to sing the team's theme song: "I'm a ramblin' wreck from Georgia Tech/And a hell of an engineer!" In 1916, the Georgia Tech football team set a world record with the astonishing score of 222 to 0. The opposing team scored the 222; the Yellowjackets scored the 0!

Atlanta Falcons player Ken Oxendine

The Georgia Tech football team
(right) plays at Dodd-Grant Field.

The Atlanta Falcons play their home
games at the Georgia Dome (below).

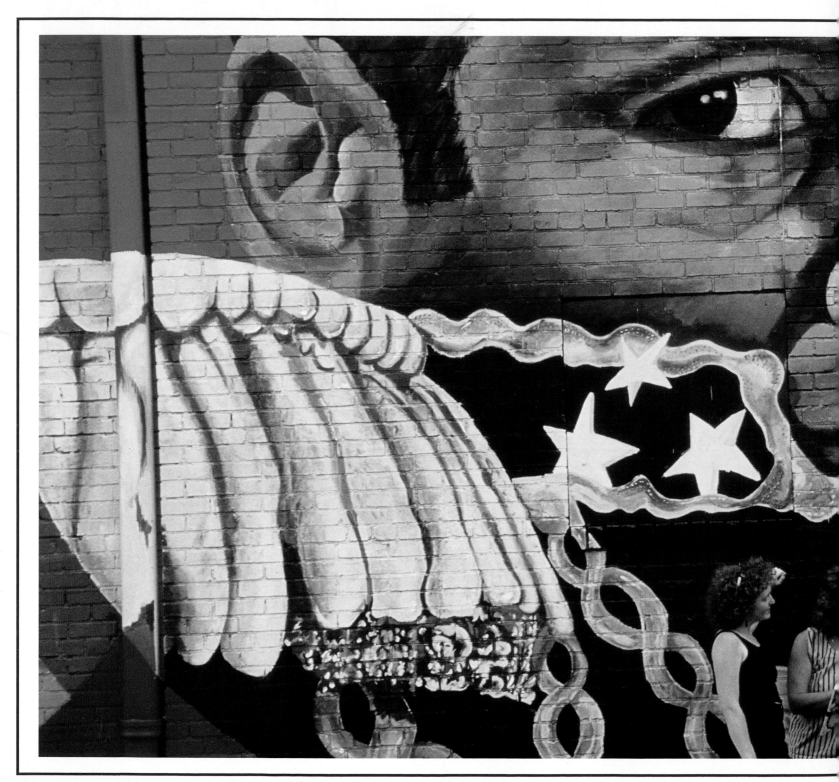

ATLANTA

Atlanta is a city that grew more by accident than by plan. Even longtime residents grumble about its maze of streets, and visitors can easily feel lost and overwhelmed. Nevertheless, the city has a logic all its own. You will discover that logic as you explore its distinct sections and neighborhoods. Whether you take the subway or travel by car, you will begin to get to know this fascinating city.

ATLANTA OUTSKIRTS

One of the most popular attractions in Greater Atlanta is Stone Mountain Park. Sprawling over 3,200 acres (1,295 hectares) of fields and woodlands, the park commemorates the Civil War. You can take a scenic railroad ride around the mountain's base to get a stunning view of the three figures on horseback carved on the mountain's north face, or you can soar to the top in a cable car where you overlook the leafy suburbs of eastern Atlanta. Information about the battle and the rock sculpture can be found at the Discovery Stone Mountain Museum.

Another Civil War encounter is remembered at the Kennesaw Mountain National Battlefield Park. Covering 2,882 acres (1,166 ha), this park marks the site of one of the battles during General Sherman's assault on Atlanta.

Confederate earthworks, trenches, and cannons are on view along a 2-mile (3-km) hiking trail. Nearby is Cheatham Hill, another battle site, with 16 miles (26 km) of trails.

The Confederate Civil War figures on this page are wearing the uniforms of a general (left), a cavalry trooper (bottom, far left to right), and an infantry private. The Union figures (left to right below) are in the uniforms of an infantry private and a cavalry major.

One of the cannons on view at the Kennesaw Mountain National Battlefield Park

A mansion in Atlanta's wealthy Buckhead section

During the summer and fall, people from all over metropolitan Atlanta flock to suburban Decatur. Decatur's chief attraction is a superb farmers' market, overflowing with fresh fruit and vegetables—corn, squash, tomatoes, melons, and, of course, bushels of delicious peaches. Decatur was named after Commodore Steven Decatur, who fought the British in the War of 1812. Recent immigrants can also find familiar foods from their homelands.

Atlanta's wealthy Buckhead section is located about 6 miles (10 km) north of Downtown. Trees line quiet streets, shading stately mansions that date back to the early twentieth century. Buckhead is sometimes called the "silk-stocking district" because most of its residents are affluent and live in luxury. In recent years, Buckhead has begun to host a lively nightlife.

The Jimmy Carter Library (left) and Presidential Center (above) are located in the Little Five Points section of Atlanta.

ALL AROUND THE TOWN

Within Atlanta lie many distinct neighborhoods, each with its own character and points of interest. The Virginia-Highland section reminds visitors of Greenwich Village in New York City. Like the Village, this Atlanta neighborhood is dotted with boutiques, restaurants, little theaters, and art galleries. Though rents are high, it is a magnet for would-be painters and writers.

South of Virginia-Highland is the section known as Little Five Points. A highlight of this neighborhood is the Jimmy Carter Library and Presidential Center. Jimmy Carter, the thirty-ninth president of the United States, was a native of Plains, Georgia. The Jimmy Carter Library is a vast storehouse of documents from Carter's years in the White House (1977–1981)—27 million pages in all. More than 1.5 million photos record Carter's life and work. Items on display range from Carter's sixth-grade report card to a magnificent Persian carpet, a gift to the president from the Shah of Iran. The Carter Center contains an exact replica of the White House's Oval Office.

In memory of its most famous resident, Dr. Martin Luther King Jr., the Sweet Auburn neighborhood is preserved as a National Historic District. Dr. King was born in a modest two-story house at 501 Auburn Avenue. King lived there until he was twelve years old, when his family moved to another house two blocks away. King's birthplace is furnished with many pieces that belonged to his family when he was growing up.

A bean-filled Atlanta "Banner" bear

The Martin Luther King Jr. Center for Nonviolent Change was created to honor and continue the work of the great civil-rights leader. The center sponsors lectures and workshops on King's philosophy of nonviolent protest. It also encourages studies on the great Indian leader Mahatma Gandhi, who pioneered nonviolent protest in the 1940s and powerfully influenced King's ideas.

Sweet Auburn's Herndon Plaza is the fully restored home of one of the district's leading figures of the nineteenth century, Alonzo F. Herndon. Born into slavery, Herndon founded the Atlanta Life Insurance Company after the Civil War. He rose to become one of the richest people in the city.

The history of Sweet Auburn comes to life at the Apex Museum. In the museum's Trolley Car Theater, visitors clamber aboard the replica of a trolley from 1900. The theater shows a twelve-minute video about Auburn Avenue, the neighborhood's main thoroughfare. Also on view at the museum are reproductions of a drugstore, a barbershop, and several other early twentieth-century buildings. Additional exhibits cover broader aspects of black history, featuring the contributions of African Americans to science, art, and music.

Two friends sitting back-to-back in an Atlanta park

The Martin Luther King Jr. Center for Nonviolent Change

Free at Last!

Every year, thousands of people pay homage to Dr. King at his grave in Freedom Plaza. King lies buried in a white marble crypt at the center of a five-tiered reflecting pool. Inscribed on the tomb are words inspired by King's most famous speech: "Free at last. Free at last. Thank God Almighty, I'm free at last."

THE HEART OF THE CITY

Piedmont Park, in the middle of Midtown Atlanta, is one of the city's most cherished public spaces.

Sprawling over 180 acres (73 ha) of grass, trees, and water, Piedmont Park rests like a jewel in the middle of Midtown Atlanta. The park is one of the city's most cherished public spaces, a playground for people of all ages. Atlantans ride bikes, jog, play softball, or feed the ducks on the park's Clara Meer Lake.

Adjoining Piedmont Park is the 30-acre (12-ha) Atlanta Botanical Gardens, with both indoor and outdoor environments to explore. The Dorothy Chapman Fuqua Conservatory specializes in tropical plants. One section is a simulated rain forest where colorful birds squawk and flutter. Another area of the Botanical Gardens shows examples of habitats in northern Georgia. Among them is a bog with rare insect-eating plants. The largest section of the park is Storza Woods, 15 acres (6 ha) of unpaved, natural forest. Here, within the boundaries of the city, live raccoons, opossums, woodchucks, and a host of songbirds.

Not far from Piedmont Park is Atlanta's Robert W. Woodruff Arts Center, the cultural hub of the city. In addition to the High Museum of Art, the complex includes the Alliance Theater, which presents several plays each year.

Symphony Hall, home to the Atlanta Symphony Orchestra, is also part of the arts center.

A smiling Atlanta schoolboy taking a break from his basketball game

One of Atlanta's most revered landmarks is the Georgia state capitol with its gilded dome. The 75-foot (23-m) dome is crowned by a robed figure representing Freedom. An ambitious program in the late 1990s has restored the Victorian-era splendor to the public areas inside the building and to the house and senate chambers. Busts of famous Georgians grace the building's vast rotunda. Sessions of the Georgia Legislature, which meets for forty days each year beginning the second week in January, are open to the public.

The gilded dome of the state capitol is crowned by a figure representing Freedom.

One Peachtree Center

The area referred to as Downtown Atlanta lies just south of the Midtown section. Despite the city's expansion into the suburbs, Downtown remains the center of retailing, business, and finance. In carpeted offices perched on the upper floors of glass-and-steel skyscrapers, corporate executives still sign multimillion-dollar agreements. The Peachtree Center Complex is a medley of office towers, stores, and convention centers, all connected by tunnels and skywalks. The complex is like a miniature city where people can live, work, and have fun without ever stepping outside.

Overlooking the front entrance to Underground Atlanta is a thirteen-story light tower, a dazzling addition to the city's skyline after dark. The city's original railway station stood at this site, but in 1930, it was replaced by a web of bridges that carried traffic

over the tracks. Below the new highways lay ghostly storefronts of nineteenth-century Atlanta. First discovered and developed in the late 1960s, Underground Atlanta declined in popularity in the early 1980s. In 1989, this underground world reopened as a labyrinth of more than 300 shops, restaurants, and nightclubs. Remembering its railroad history, Underground Atlanta sits across the railroad tracks from the site of the original Western & Atlantic terminal with the "Zero Milepost."

You can get a glimpse behind the scenes of 24-hour cable news when you explore the CNN Center in Downtown

Atlanta. Be part of the audience on *Talk Back Live*, or try delivering your own late-breaking news story while video cameras roll. The most spectacular feature of the CNN

building is a dizzying eighty-story escalator.

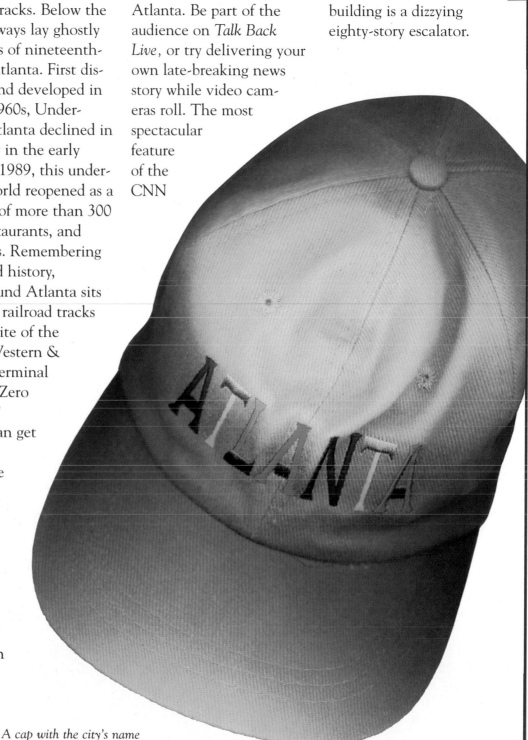

A cap with the city's name embroidered on the front

The living and the dead are comfortable companions at Oakland Cemetery. Joggers run up and down the rows of headstones, and picnickers sit at tables beneath the trees. Opened in 1850, Oakland Cemetery has some 34,000 graves, as well as two monuments to the Confederate soldiers who died in the Civil War. The carving of headstones was a fine art in the nineteenth century. Stones at Oakland Cemetery are adorned with angels, lambs, flowers, doves, wreaths, and

heavenly harps. A life-sized statue marks the grave of real-estate tycoon Jasper Newton Smith. According to legend, Smith ordered his likeness made so he could keep an eye on the comings and goings around him in death as he did in life.

At the heart of Downtown Atlanta is Centennial Olympic Park, the newest park in the city. Thousands of well-wishers donated money to establish this park where the 1996 Olympic Games were held. The names of these donors

are inscribed on half a million commemorative bricks that form a network of walkways through the park. Five stone "quilts" border the park, telling the story of the Games in carved words and pictures. The Quilt of Remembrance honors the victims of the bomb that exploded during the Olympic festivities.

These children portray, in part, Atlanta's ethnic diversity.

At the Ring Fountain, visitors to the park play and laugh in the cooling spray. They marvel at the intricate jets of water that form five interlocking rings. They gaze at the flags of twenty-three nations that have hosted the modern Olympic Games. The fountain reminds them of the summer when the world came to Atlanta. Every day, through industry, the media, sports, and the arts, Atlanta reaches out to the world.

Crowds enjoying the games at the 1996 Olympics

A Land of Make-Believe

When the Fox Theater opened in 1929, going to the movies meant stepping into a world of enchantment. The Fox was designed to look like a Moorish-Egyptian palace, complete with domes and minarets. In the ornate lobby, fountains splashed and goldfish swam in tiled pools. The ceiling of the auditorium sparkled with stars, and the sequined curtain bore scenes of galloping Arab horsemen. Restored to its former splendor, the Fox Theater now hosts dance companies, variety shows, Broadway musicals, and the Atlanta Opera.

FAMOUS LANDMARKS

The tombstone of Confederate soldier W. H. Clay in Oakland Cemetery, with the Confederate Monument in the background

The Margaret Mitchell House and Museum

The Fernbank Museum of Natural History

Stone Mountain Park
This park is a popular recreation area in the eastern outskirts of Atlanta. On the north face of Stone Mountain are carved the figures of three Confederate leaders.

Oakland Cemetery
This cemetery, which opened in 1850, has more than 34,000 graves. Separate sections for African Americans and Jews can be observed, dating back to the nineteenth century.

Georgia State Capitol
Completed in 1889, this impressive building is topped by a 75-foot (23-m) gilded dome. Sessions of the legislature are open to the public.

Martin Luther King Jr. Center for Nonviolent Change
Founded to encourage social change through nonviolent action, the center offers lectures and workshops year-round. Dr. King's tomb is on the grounds, surrounded by a five-tiered reflecting pool and lit by an eternal flame.

Margaret Mitchell House and Museum
Between 1927 and 1932, Margaret Mitchell wrote *Gone with the Wind* in her first-floor apartment in this modest 10-unit building. Exhibits depict Mitchell's life and the writing of her classic novel.

Jimmy Carter Library and Museum
The Jimmy Carter Library houses the presidential papers and other documents of the nation's chief executive. The museum contains memorabilia on Carter's life from childhood through his post-White House years.

High Museum of Art
With four floors of galleries, the High is the biggest art museum in Atlanta. Its collections contain some 10,000 paintings and sculptures from the United States, Europe, Africa, and Asia.

Fernbank Museum of Natural History
Dinosaurs, minerals, birds, and stars—the natural world is revealed in all its facets at this enthralling museum. One popular section—"A Walk through Time in Georgia"—features eighteen galleries of displays on Georgia habitats, present and past.

The Wren's Nest, home of author Joel Chandler Harris

The Georgia state capitol

The Dorothy Chapman Fuqua Conservatory in the Atlanta Botanical Gardens

Atlanta History Center

The history of Atlanta, the Civil War, and Georgia folk crafts are among the permanent exhibits at this museum complex, which includes a nineteenth-century farmhouse complex where visitors can participate in hands-on demonstrations of weaving, candle-making, and even sheep-shearing. Visitors tour Swan House, an elegant early 1900s mansion, and look for the swan motif that appears in every room.

Martin Luther King Jr. Birthplace

This two-story Queen Anne-style home has been fully restored to look as it did during Dr. King's early childhood.

Centennial Olympic Park

Names and messages on brick pathways commemorate the thousands of people who donated money to create this downtown park. The park hosts concerts and festivals and is a gathering place for Atlantans of all ages.

Atlanta Botanical Gardens

This extensive series of habitats covers 30 acres (12 ha) adjoining Atlanta's Piedmont Park. In addition to the carefully planted gardens, 15 acres (6 ha) are devoted to Storza Woods, an island of wilderness in the midst of Downtown Atlanta.

World of Coca-Cola Museum

This museum traces the history of the world's most popular soft drink. At Club Coca-Cola, visitors can sample thirty-eight Coke beverages, many of which are sold only overseas.

Wren's Nest

This historic house was the home of Joel Chandler Harris, best-known for his tales of Uncle Remus, Bre'r Rabbit, and Bre'r Fox. Harris gathered most of the stories from slaves on his family's plantation and recorded them for future generations. He lived at the Wren's Nest from 1881 to 1908.

FAST FACTS

POPULATION

	1990
City	394,017
Metropolitan Area	2,959,950

AREA

City	132 square miles (342 sq km)
Metropolitan Area	6,126 square miles (15,866 sq km)

LOCATION   Atlanta is located in northern Georgia. Its Downtown is 6 miles (10 km) east of the banks of the Chattahoochee River. It lies in the foothills of the Blue Ridge Mountains, at an altitude of 1,050 feet (320 m) above sea level.

CLIMATE   Atlanta has warm, humid summers and mild winters. The average July temperature is 79 degrees Fahrenheit (26° Celsius), and the average temperature in January is 41° F. (5° C). The city receives about 51 inches (130 cm) of precipitation (rain, sleet, and snow) each year.

ECONOMY   Atlanta's economy is largely based on service industries including wholesale and retail sales, health care, research, and government services. Manufactured goods include processed foods, transportation equipment, tobacco products, textiles, and electronics.

CHRONOLOGY

1782
English explorers reach the Cherokee village of Standing Peach Tree on the Chattahoochee River.

1813
During the War of 1812, the U.S. Army establishes Fort Peach Tree as a defense against the British.

1837
Stephen H. Long, an engineer for the Western & Atlantic Railroad, selects the site for the southern terminus of the line.

1843
Terminus is renamed Marthasville.

1845
Marthasville is renamed Atlanta; the arrival of the Western & Atlantic Railroad completes a rail nexus opening to the ports of Savannah and Charleston, the markets of north Georgia.

1861
Georgia secedes from the Union and joins the Confederate States of America; Civil War begins.

1864
Union general William Tecumseh Sherman captures Atlanta after several bloody battles; Sherman and his men burn the city.

1865
The Confederacy is defeated; Civil War ends; Atlantans begin to rebuild their city.

1868
Atlanta becomes the capital of Georgia.

1886
Atlanta pharmacist John S. Pemberton markets Coca-Cola as a headache remedy.

1895
The Cotton State and International Exposition is held at what is now Piedmont Park; Booker T. Washington delivers his "Atlanta Compromise" speech at opening ceremonies.

1917
Fire destroys 73 square blocks in Atlanta.

A face-painting artist at an Atlanta fair

1936
Margaret Mitchell publishes *Gone with the Wind,* the basis for the 1939 Civil War film.

1952
Atlanta annexes 81 square miles (210 sq km) of surrounding suburbs.

1957
Dr. Martin Luther King Jr. founds the Southern Christian Leadership Conference (SCLC) to promote African-American civil rights.

1961
Atlanta's public schools become racially integrated.

1966
The Milwaukee Braves baseball team moves to Atlanta.

1974
Maynard Jackson is elected Atlanta's first African-American mayor.

1979
Atlanta inaugurates MARTA (Metropolitan Atlanta Rapid Transit Authority).

1988
Atlanta hosts the Democratic National Convention.

1996
Atlanta hosts the Centennial Olympic Games.

1998
Turner Field opens at former Olympic Stadium.

ATLANTA

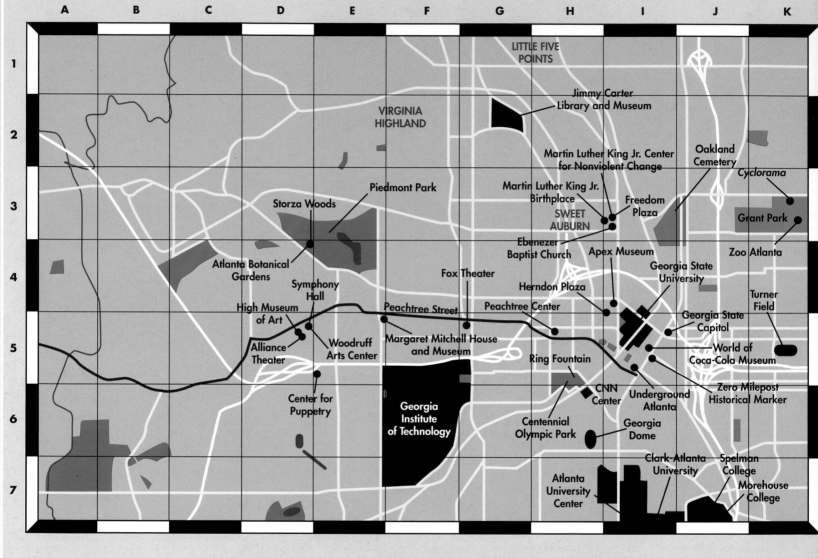

A B C D E F G H I J K

1
LITTLE FIVE
POINTS

2
VIRGINIA
HIGHLAND
Jimmy Carter
Library and Museum
Oakland
Cemetery
Cyclorama

3
Piedmont Park
Storza Woods
Martin Luther King Jr. Center
for Nonviolent Change
Martin Luther King Jr.
Birthplace
Freedom
Plaza
Grant Park
SWEET
AUBURN
Ebenezer
Baptist Church
Apex Museum
Zoo Atlanta

4
Atlanta Botanical
Gardens
Fox Theater
Georgia State
University
Symphony
Hall
Herndon Plaza
High Museum
of Art
Peachtree Street
Peachtree Center
Turner
Field

5
Alliance
Theater
Woodruff
Arts Center
Margaret Mitchell House
and Museum
Georgia State
Capitol
World of
Coca-Cola Museum
Ring Fountain
Zero Milepost
Historical Marker

6
Center for
Puppetry
Georgia
Institute
of Technology
CNN
Center
Underground
Atlanta
Centennial
Olympic Park
Georgia
Dome

7
Atlanta
University
Center
Clark-Atlanta
University
Spelman
College
Morehouse
College

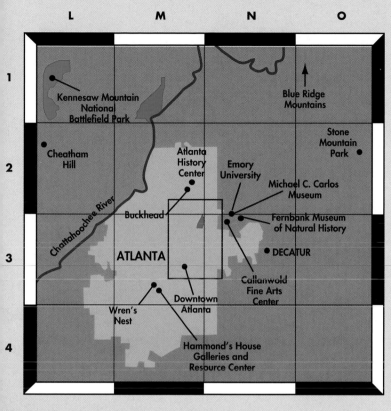

ATLANTA & SURROUNDINGS

GLOSSARY

affluent: Wealthy and privileged

archives: Collection of documents

bas-relief: Sculpture in which figures are slightly raised from a flat background

crypt: Stone tomb

discrimination: Unjust behavior toward others based on particular characteristics

eclipse: To cast into darkness, to overshadow

emulate: Imitate

ingenious: Clever

ironic: Surprising and unexpected results

irresistible: Too good to pass up

labyrinth: Maze

legacy: Parting gift

minaret: Moorish tower

mobile: Sculpture with movable, hanging parts

outcropping: Jutting projection of rock

qualms: Twinges, reservations

replica: Exact re-creation

secede: Break away from

thoroughfare: Major street

Picture Identifications

Cover: Atlanta Botanical Gardens and the Dorothy Chapman Fuqua Conservatory with smiling girls in foreground
Page 1: Model posing as Scarlett O'Hara, the main character in *Gone with the Wind*
Pages 4–5: Children playing in the Centennial Olympic Park Ring Fountain
Pages 8–9: "Southern Belles" in an Atlanta Fourth of July parade
Pages 18–19: Atlantans evacuating the city before the arrival of Union troops led by General William Tecumseh Sherman
Pages 32–33: Lovely gardens at the Carter Presidential Center
Pages 42–43: A mural in Little Five Points honoring African Americans

Photo Credits ©

Tony Stone Images, Inc. — Ken Biggs, cover (background)
Photo Edit — David Young-Wolff, cover (foreground), 54; Myrleen Ferguson Cate, 14, 48; Michael Newman, 16 (left), 51 (right); Robert W. Ginn, 16 (right), 17, 49 (bottom), 56 (left); Bachmann, 52 (left)
Bob Krist — 1, 7, 6, 8–9, 12–13, 15 (bottom), 42–43, 59
KK&A, Ltd. — 3, 21 (peaches), 22 (left), 24 (bottom), 26 (left), 37 (right), 39 (right), 44 (soldiers), 53, 60, 61
New England Stock Photo — Jean Higgins, 4–5; Andre Jenny, 11 (right), 31
Courtesy Olympic Committee — 6 (left)
Aristock, Inc. — Craig M. Tanner, 6 (right), 51 (left); Cotten Alston, 10, 46–47, 56 (bottom right); Jean Higgins, 15 (top); Michael Siede, 34; The Write Idea, Inc., 35 (bottom); Ron Sherman, 38, 45; Robb Helfrick, 44 (bottom middle); Richard T. Bryant, 55 (bottom); Michael Worthy, 57 (left)
Cameramann International, Ltd. — 11 (left), 50
Liaison Agency — 20, 22 (right), 24 (top), 26–27, 29 (bottom), 30 (left); Eric Sander, 13, 41–42; The New York Historical Society, 25 (top); Fred Charles, 55 (top)
Stock Montage, Inc. — 18–19, 27 (top and bottom right), 28
North Wind Picture Archives — 21 (left)
North Wind Pictures — 25 (both pictures)
Milton Fullman — 25 (bottom), 56 (top right)
Courtesy of the Atlanta History Center — 29 (top)
Bettmann/CORBIS — 30 (right), 39 (left)
Dave G. Houser — 32–33, 49 (top)
Allsport — 40 (left)
Icon Sports Media, Inc. — Dale Zanine, 41 (top)
Salvino, Inc. — 47 (right)
SuperStock — 57 (right); Hidekazu Nishibata, 35 (top); Timothy Hursley, 52 (right)
Unicorn Stock Photos — Andre Jenny, 36, 57 (middle); Jean Higgins, 37 (left), 46 (bottom)

INDEX

TO FIND OUT MORE

BOOKS

Atlanta 1996: Official Commemorative Book of the Centennial Olympic Games. Emeryville, Calif.: Woodford Press, 1996.

Black, Denise. *Around Atlanta with Children: A Guide for Family Activities.* Marietta, Georgia: Longstreet Press, 1997.

Goodman, Michael E. *Atlanta Falcons.* Mankato, Minn.: Creative Education, 1997.

Goodman, Michael E. *The History of the Atlanta Braves.* Mankato, Minn.: Creative Education, 1997.

Green, Carl R. *The Civil War Soldier at Atlanta.* Mankato, Minn.: Capstone Press, 1991.

Hacker, Randy. *Ladybird Guide to the Centennial Olympic Games.* East Rutherford, N.J.: Ladybird Books, 1996.

Hauser, Pierre. *Community Builders 1877–1895: From the End of Reconstruction to the Atlanta Compromise.* New York: Chelsea House Publishers, 1996.

Knorr, Roseanne. *Kidding Around Atlanta: A Fun Filled, Fact Packed Travel & Activity Book.* Santa Fe: John Muir Publications, 1997.

Larson, Judy L. *American Paintings at the High Museum of Art.* New York: Hudson Hills Press, 1997.

McKissack, Patricia. *Martin Luther King Jr.: Man of Peace.* Springfield, N.J.: Enslow Publishers Inc., 1991.

Rambeck, Richard. *Atlanta Hawks.* Mankato, Minn.: Creative Education, 1998

ONLINE SITES

Atlanta Braves
http://www.atlantabraves.com/
The official online home of the Atlanta Braves, this site has information on everything you want to know about this National League baseball franchise, including the players, the schedule, tours of Turner Field, up-to-date news, fan connections, how to order Braves merchandise, team charities, Atlanta attractions, and more.

Atlanta Guidebook
http://clever.net/qms/atl-page.htm
All you want to know about the city of Atlanta and surrounding counties, including links to general information, maps, hotels, restaurants, attractions, sports, arts and culture, schools, entertainment, and more.

Gateway to Atlanta
http://www.posted-on-inter.net/travel.html
This site has many links to transportation information, accommodations, points of interest, sports, and much more.

Jimmy Carter Library and Museum
http://carterlibrary.galileo.peachnet.edu/
All about this presidential library and museum, with links to biographies about Jimmy and Rosalynn Carter, manuscript collections, research, a kid's corner, an events calendar, the Carter Center, and more.

Martin Luther King, Jr. National Historic Site
http://www.nps.gov/malu/
A description of King's birthplace in Sweet Auburn and the nearby Ebenezer Baptist Church, where King, his father, and his grandfather were pastors.

Stone Mountain Park
http://www.stonemountainpark.org/main.html
The largest bas-relief sculpture on earth depicts three leaders of the Confederacy: President Jefferson Davis and Generals Stonewall Jackson and Robert E. Lee. The site has links to the Stone Mountain Museum, the Lasershow, and much more.

ABOUT THE AUTHOR

Deborah Kent grew up in Little Falls, New Jersey, and received a B.A. in English from Oberlin College. She earned a master's degree from Smith College School for Social Work. After working for four years at the University Settlement House in New York City, she moved to San Miguel de Allende in central Mexico. There she wrote her first young-adult novel, *Belonging*. Ms. Kent is the author of many titles in the Children's Press Cities of the World series. She lives in Chicago with her husband, author R. Conrad Stein, and their daughter Janna.